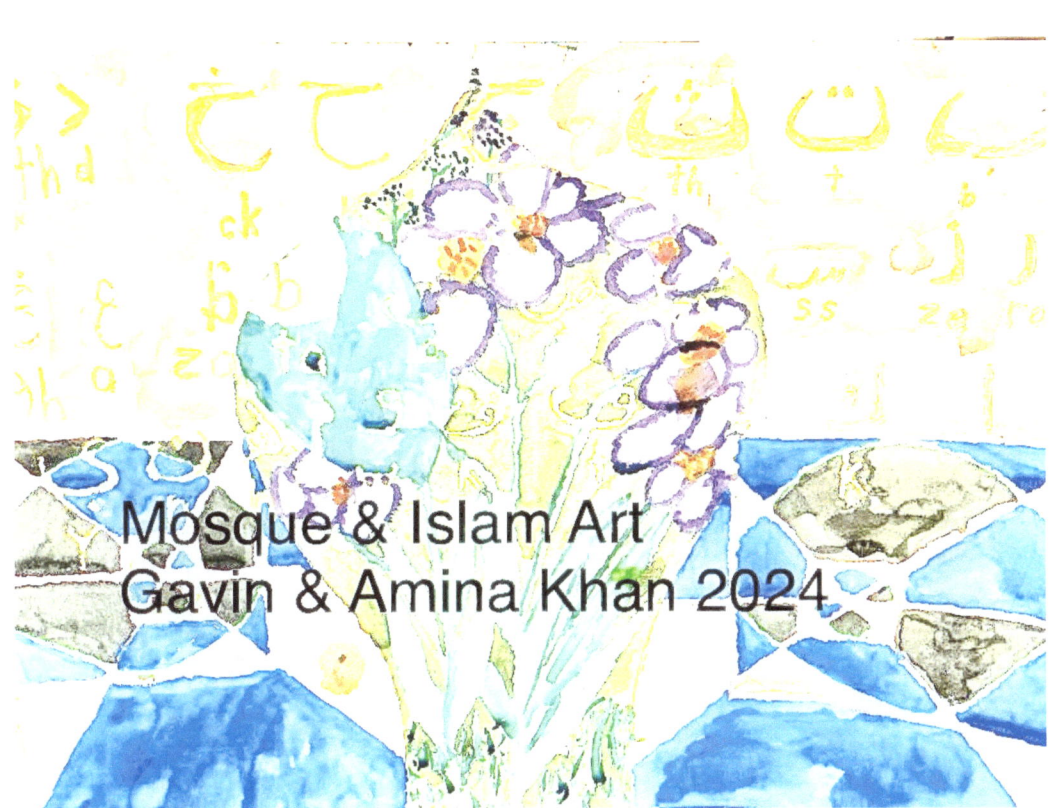

Mosque & Islam Art
Gavin & Amina Khan 2024

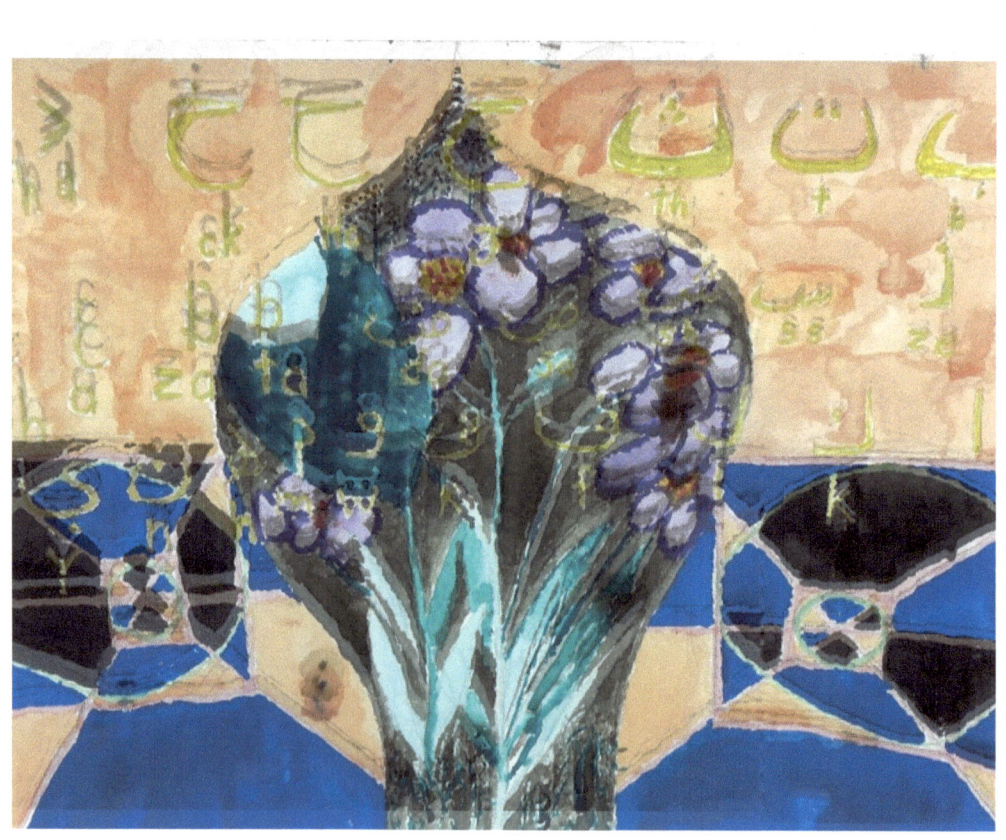

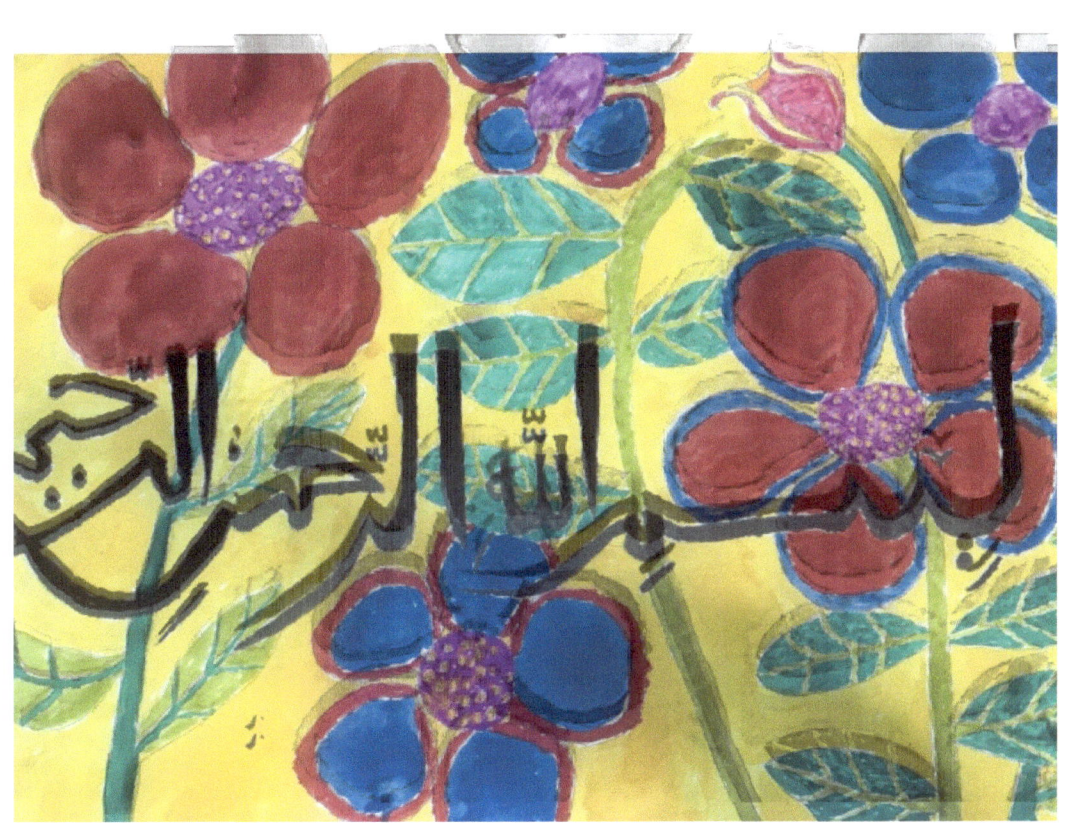

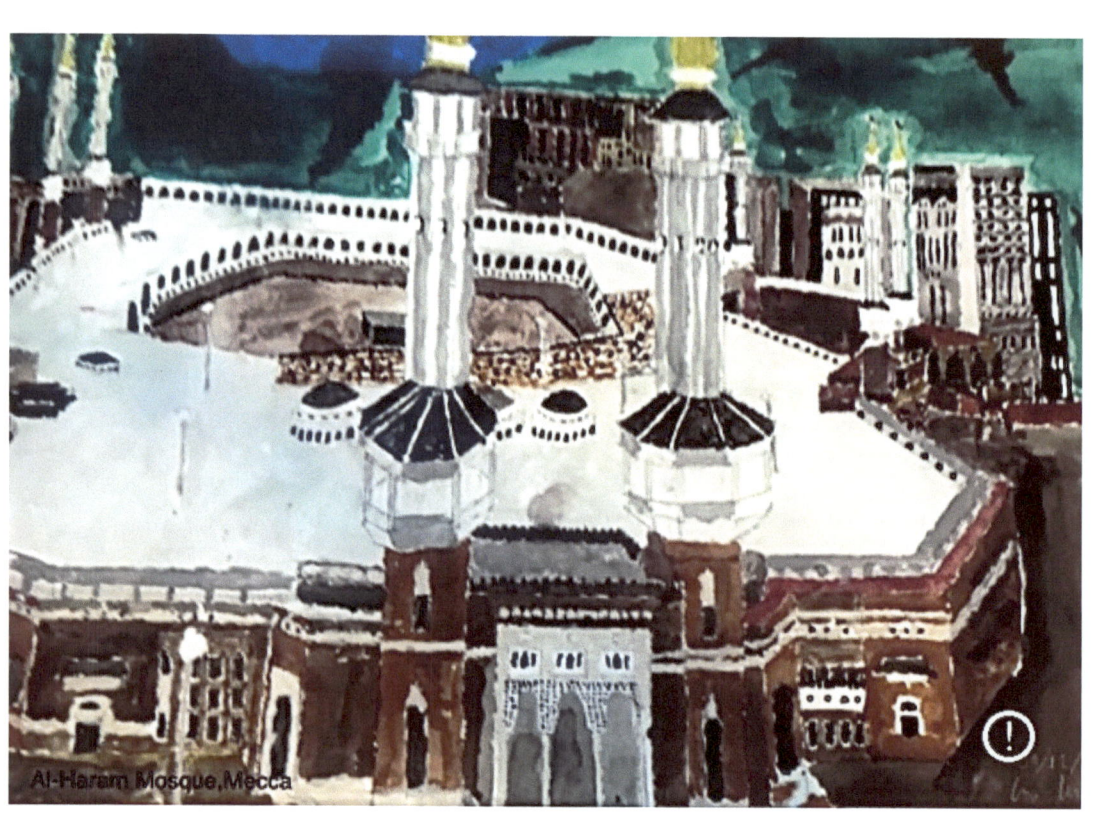

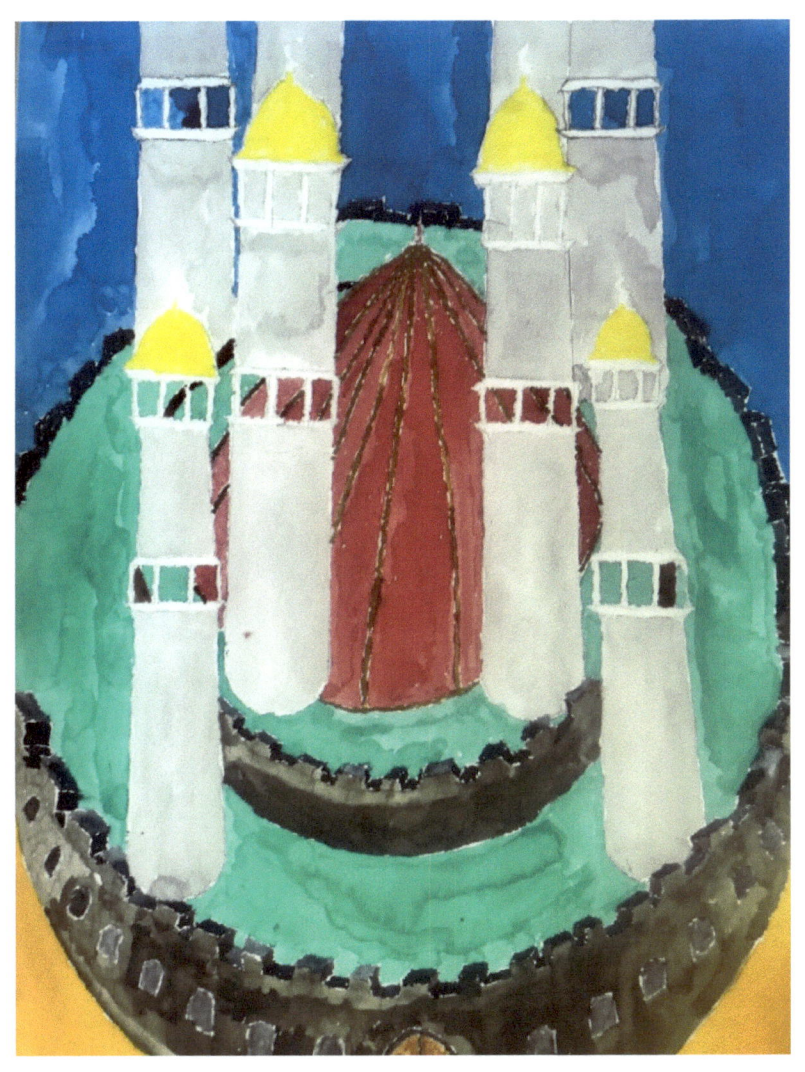

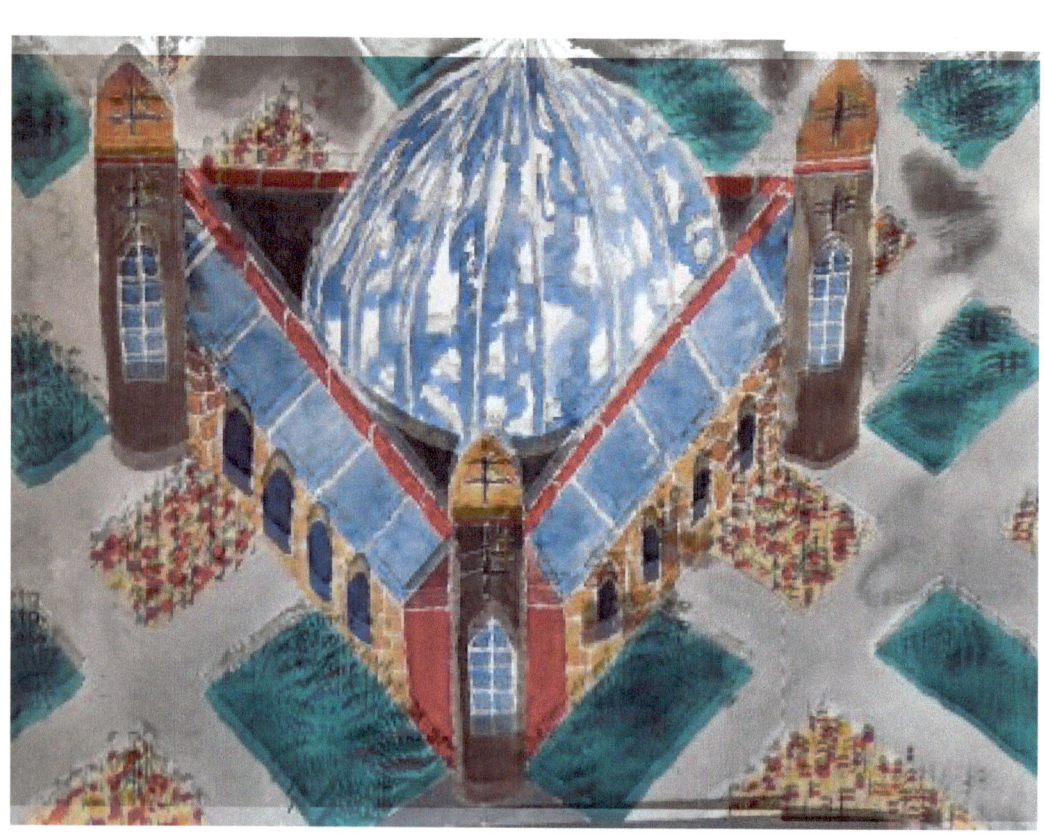

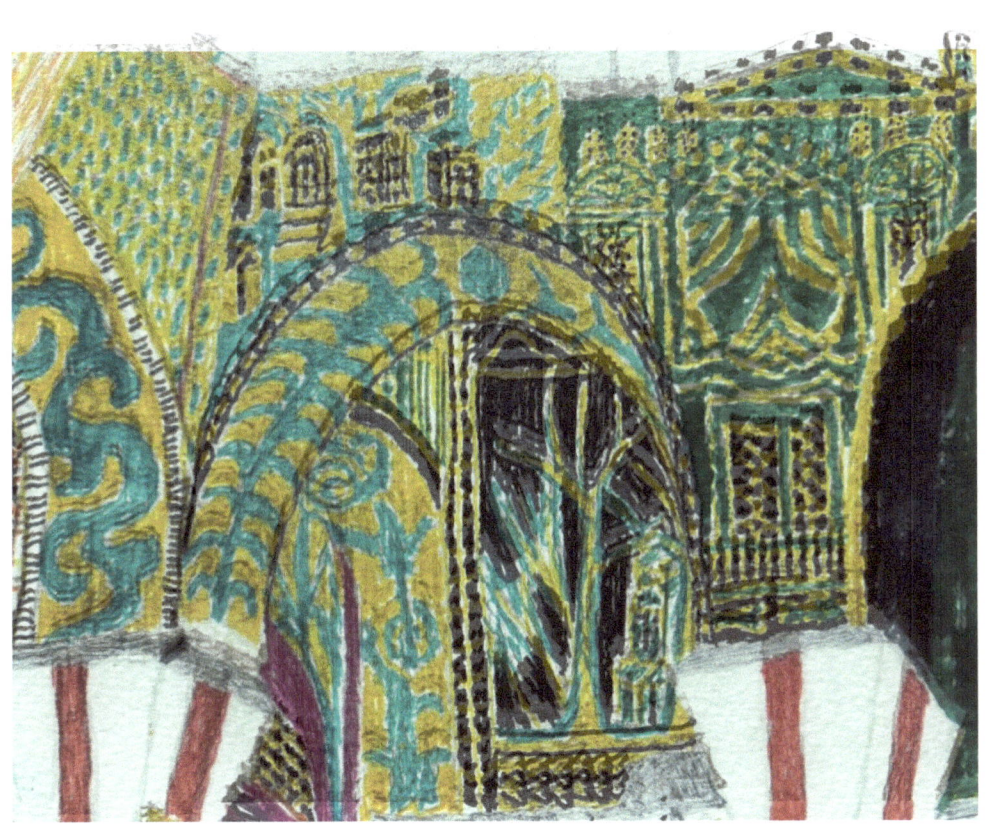

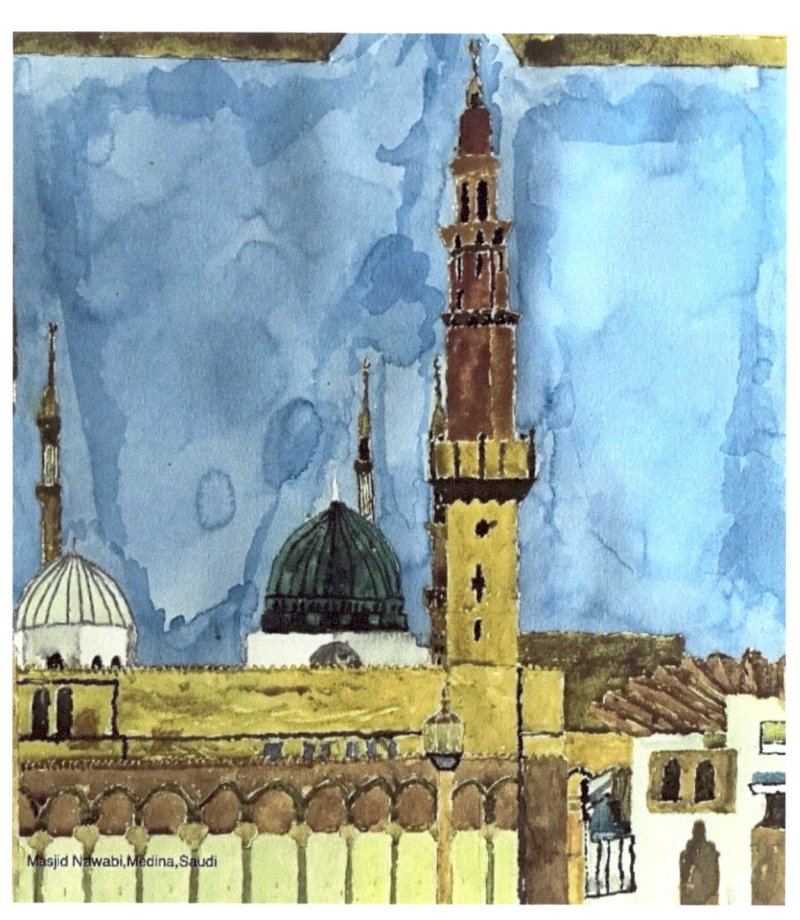

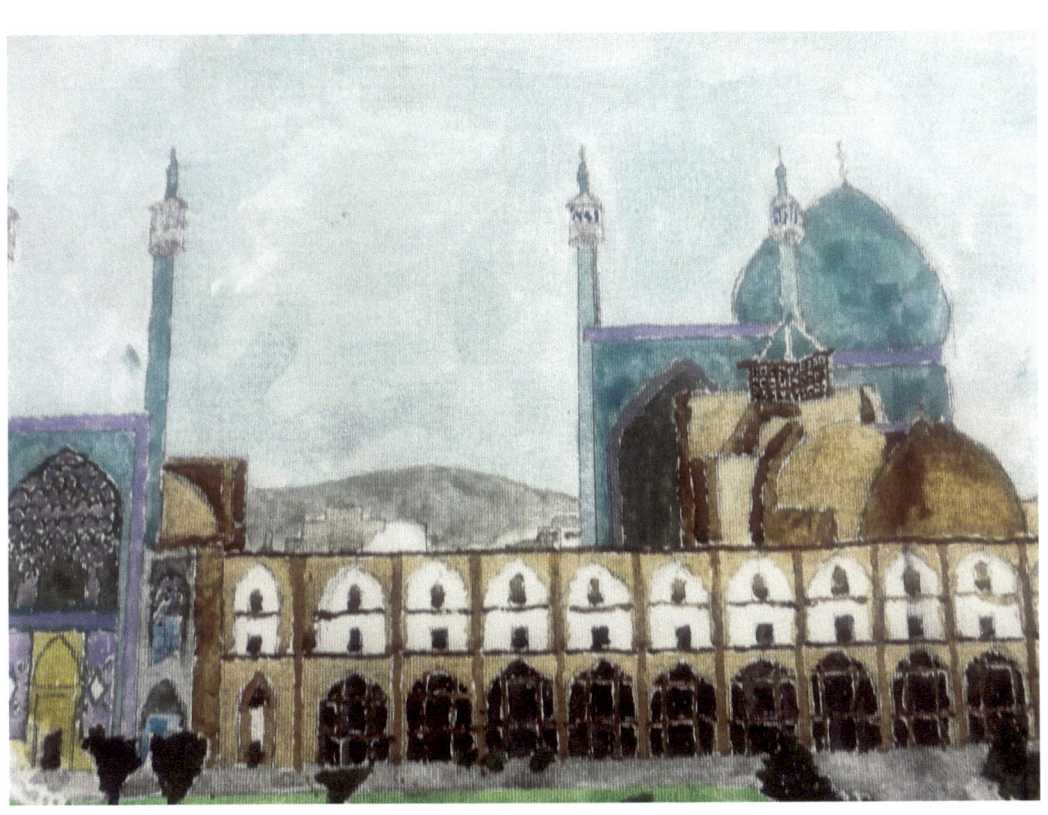

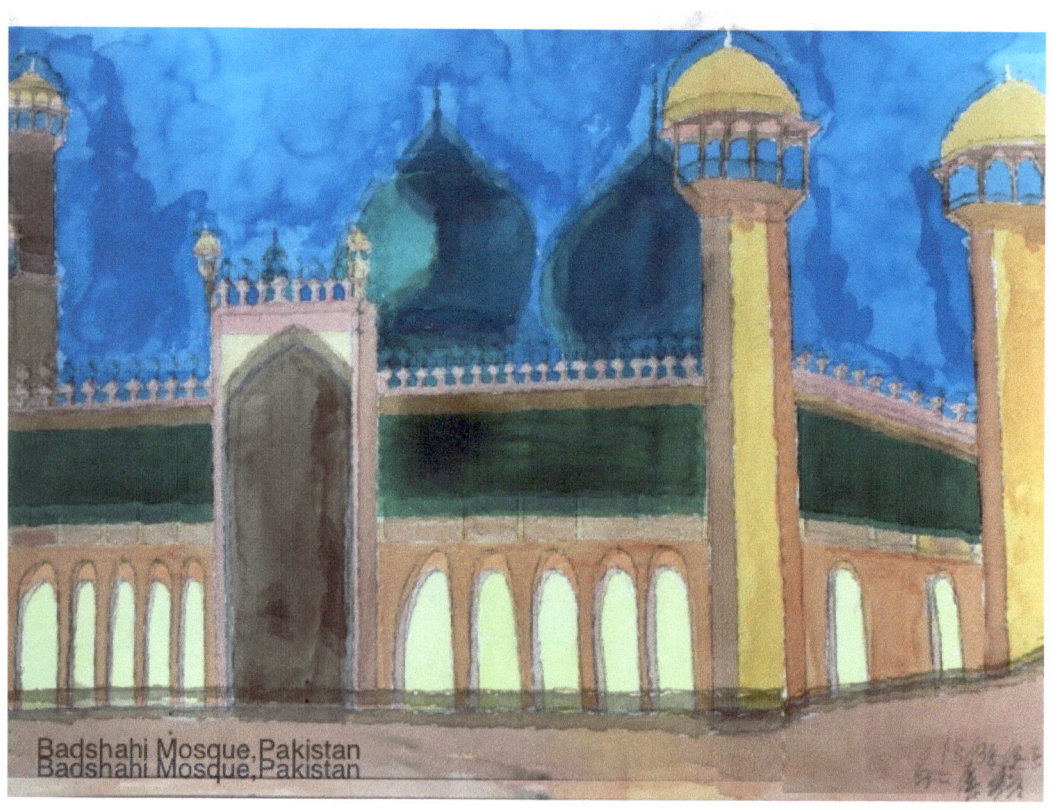

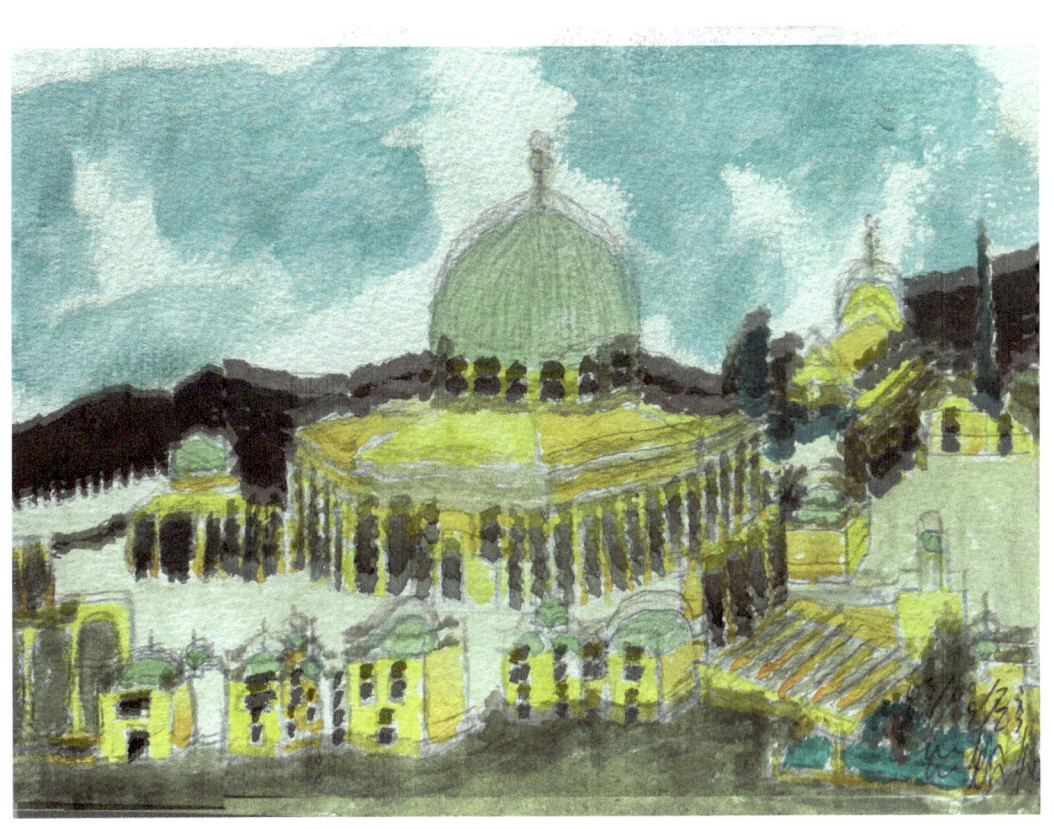

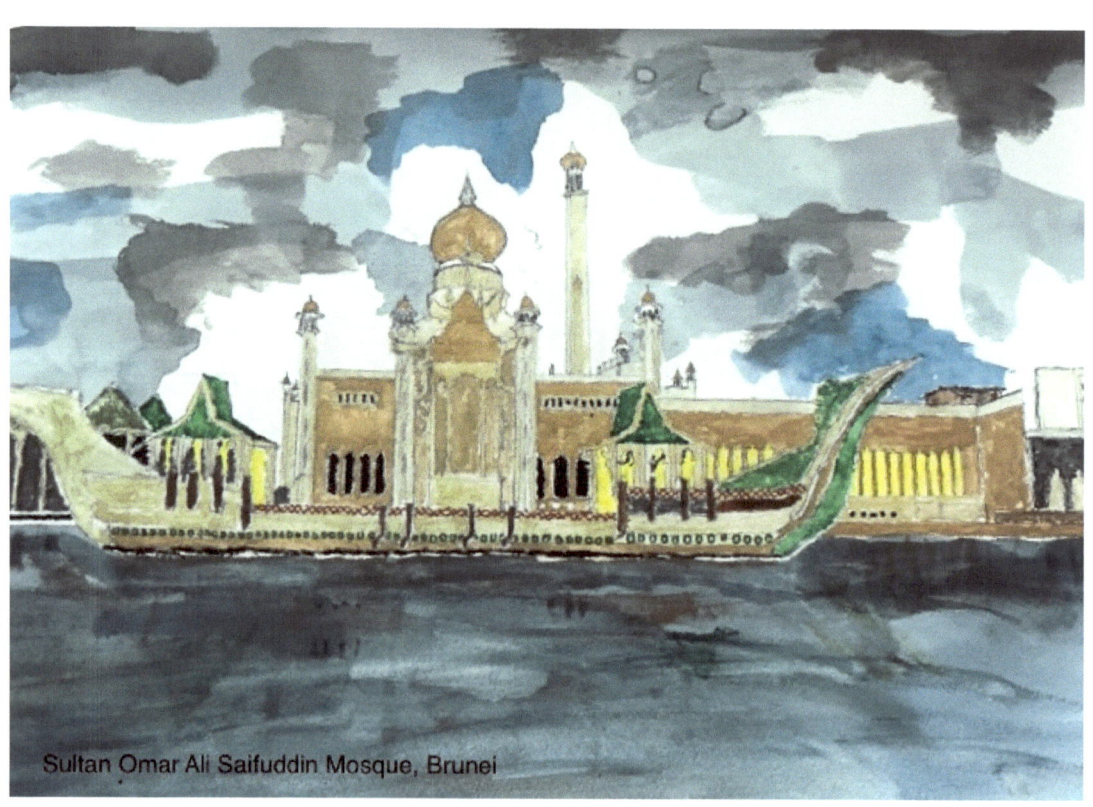
Sultan Omar Ali Saifuddin Mosque, Brunei

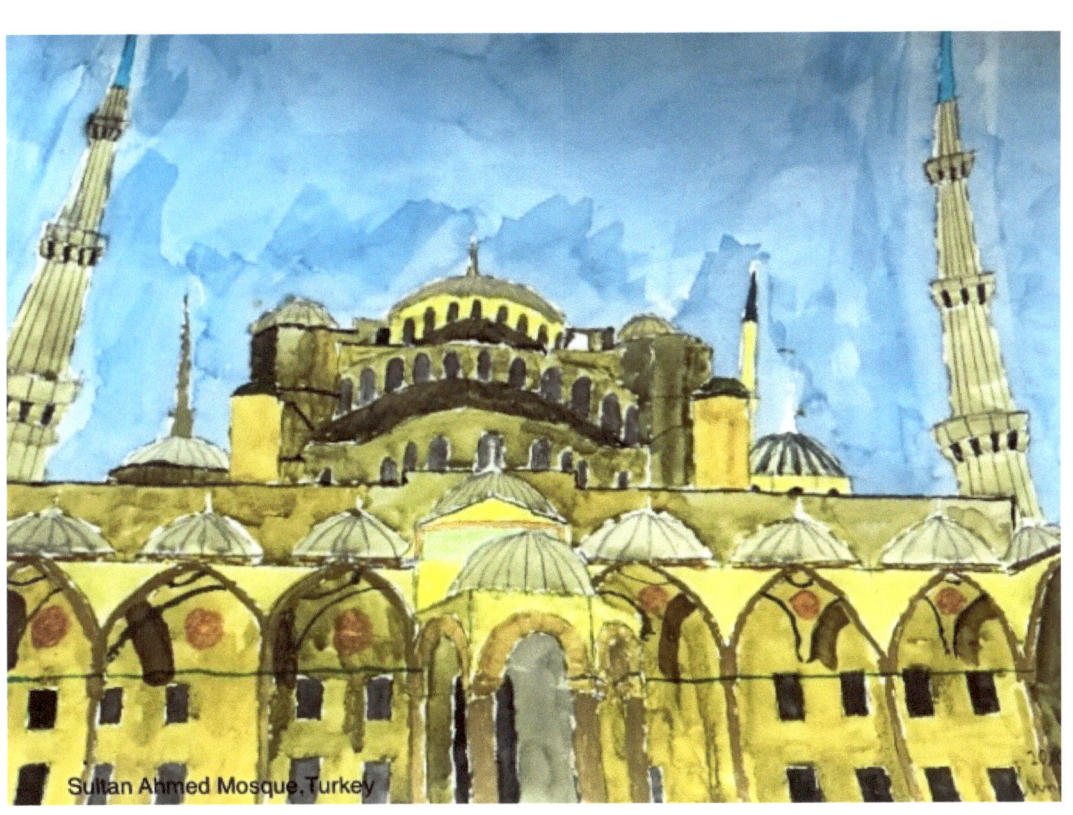
Sultan Ahmed Mosque, Turkey

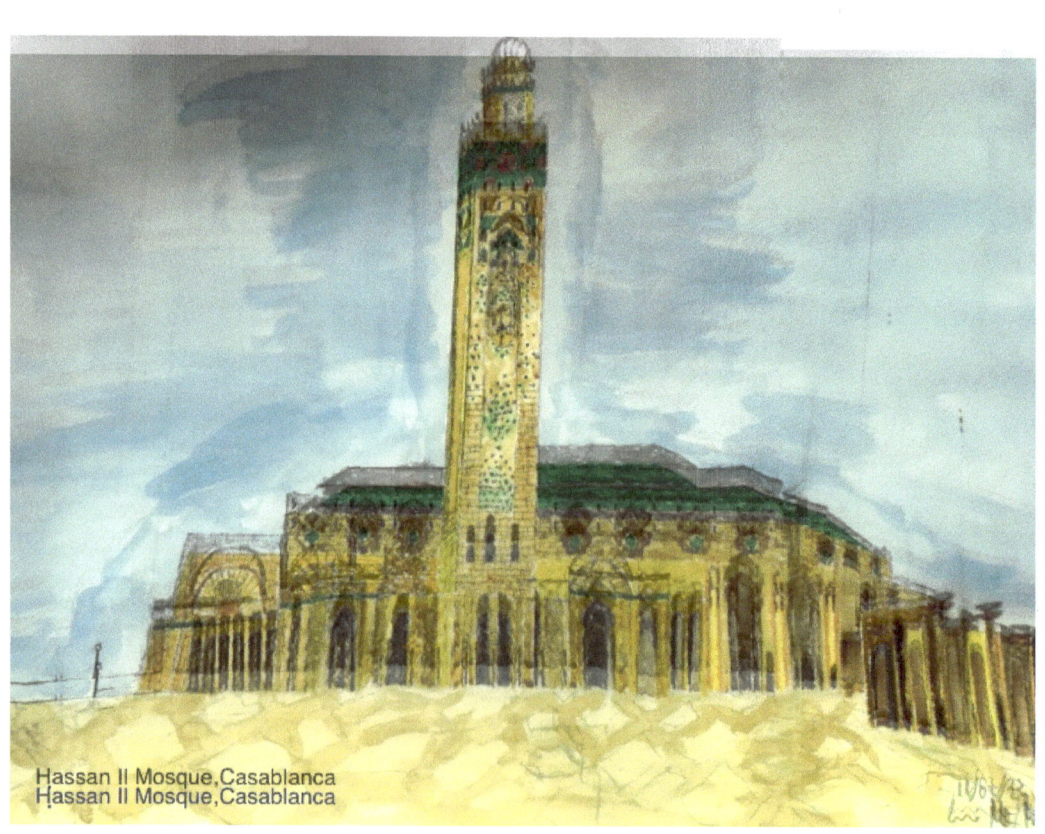

Hassan II Mosque, Casablanca
Hassan II Mosque, Casablanca

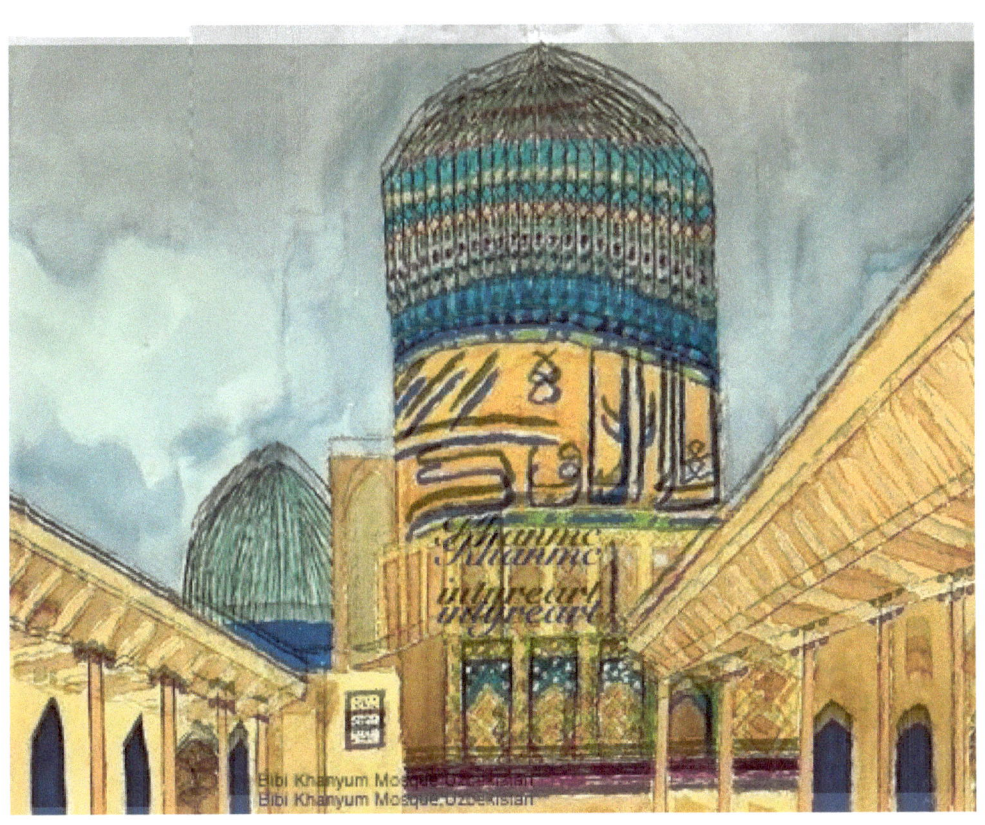

Bibi Khanyum Mosque, Uzbekistan

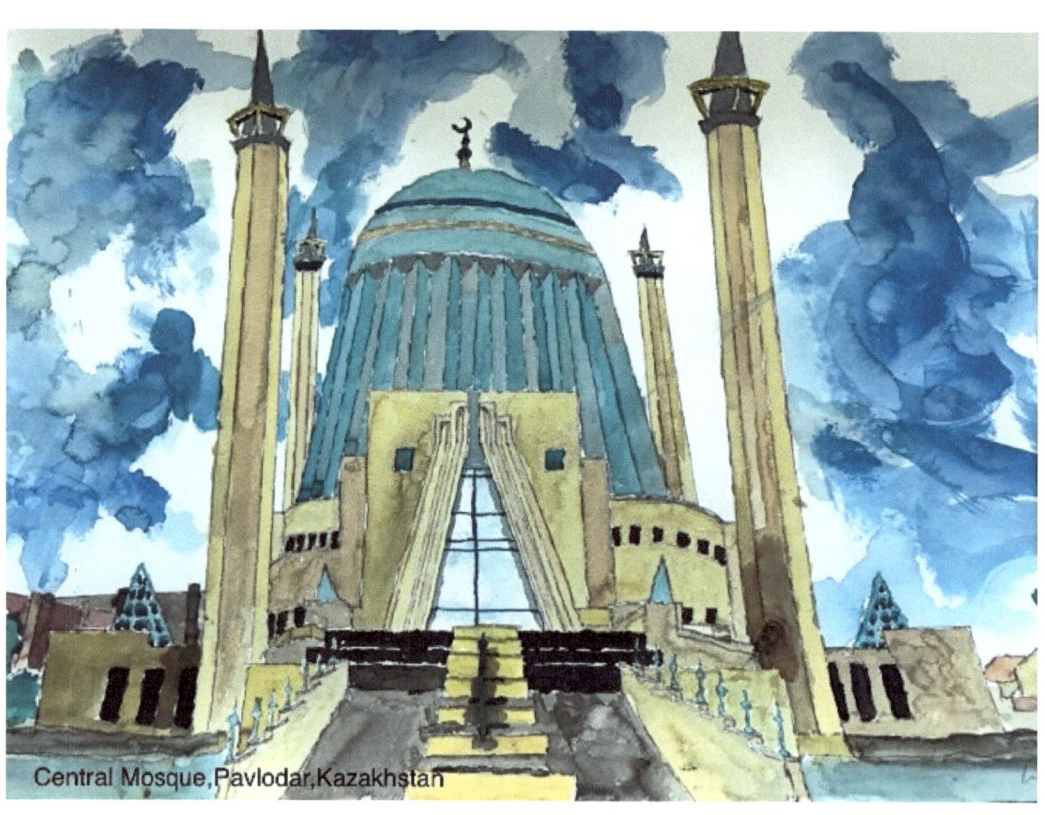

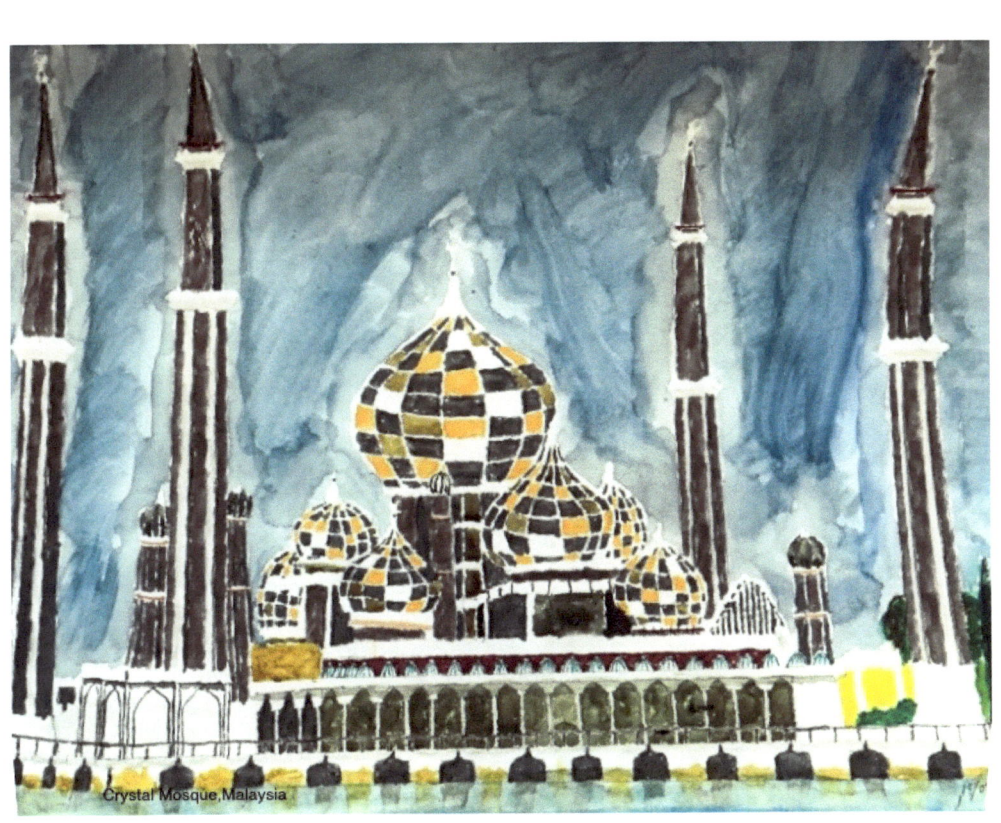
Crystal Mosque, Malaysia

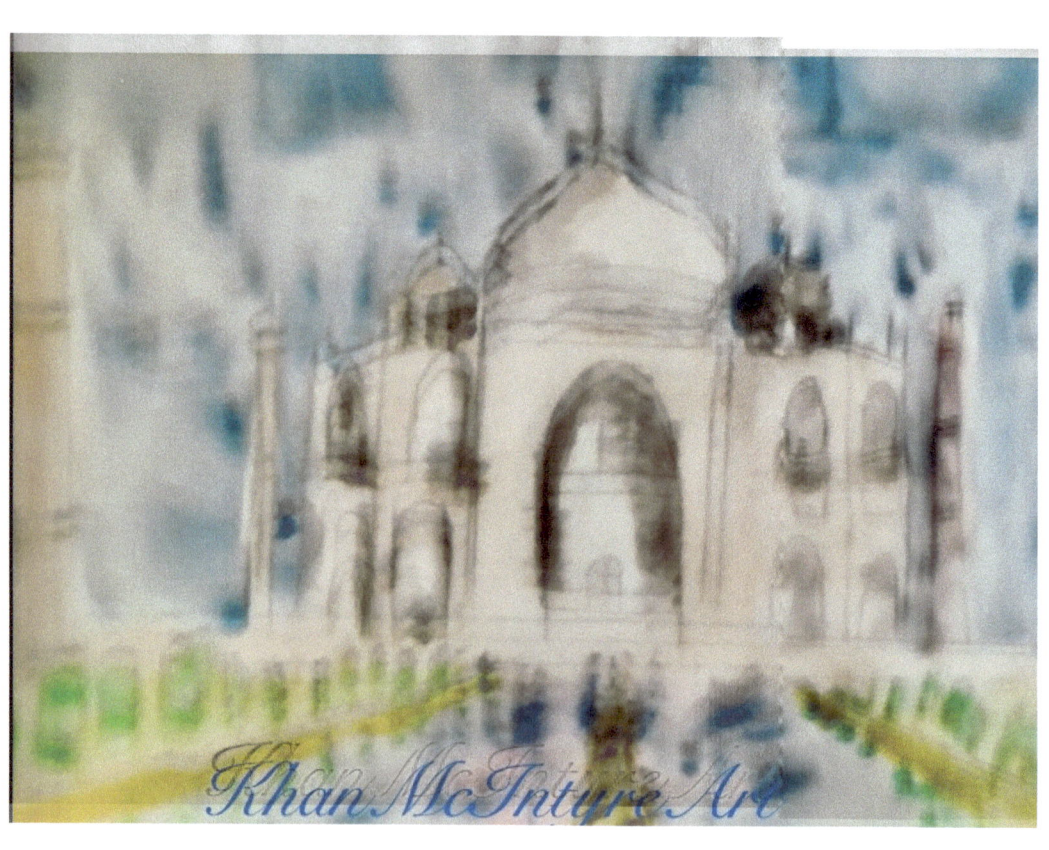

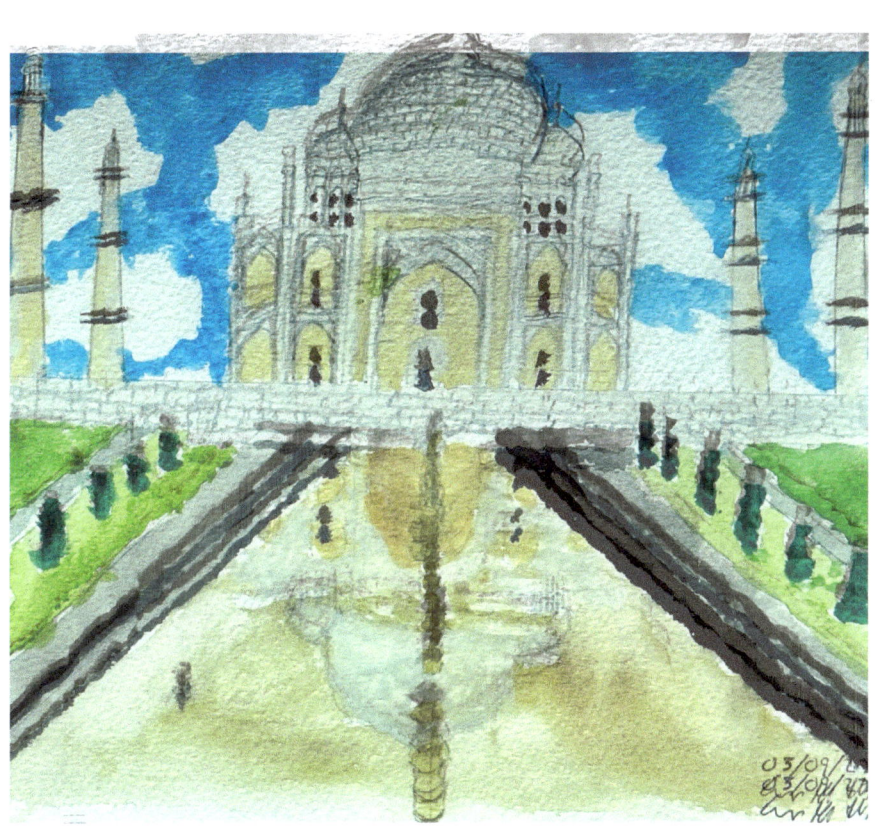

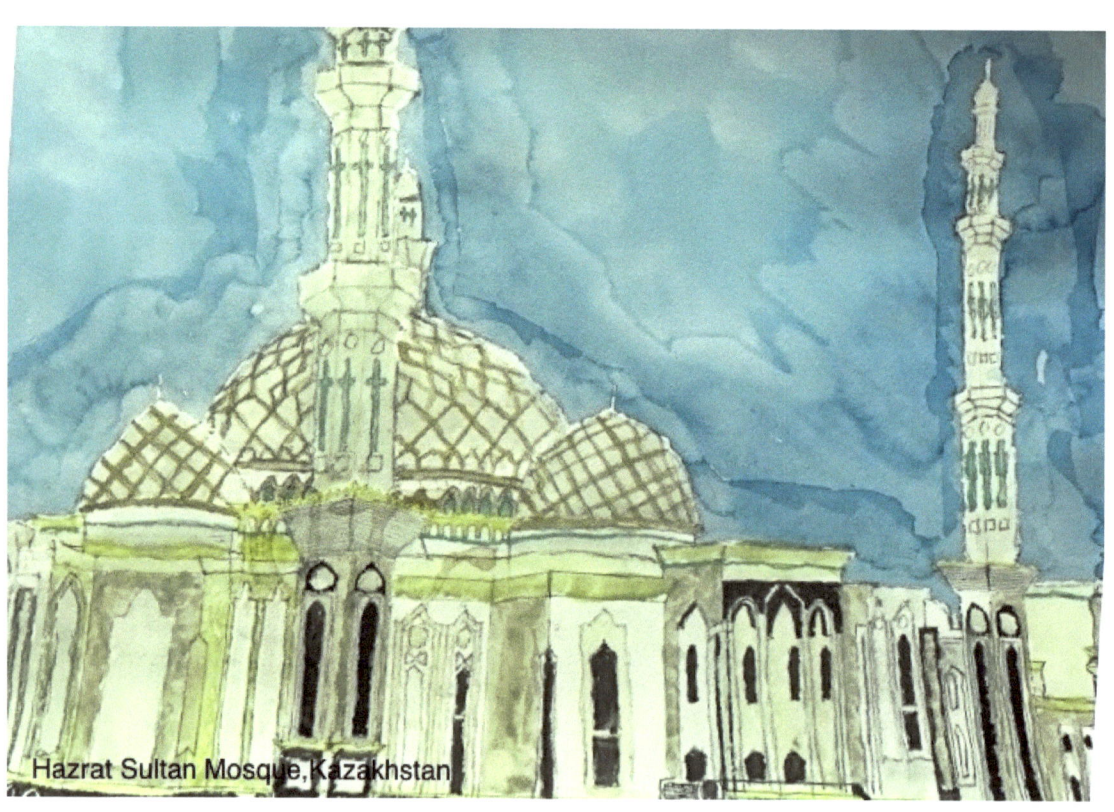

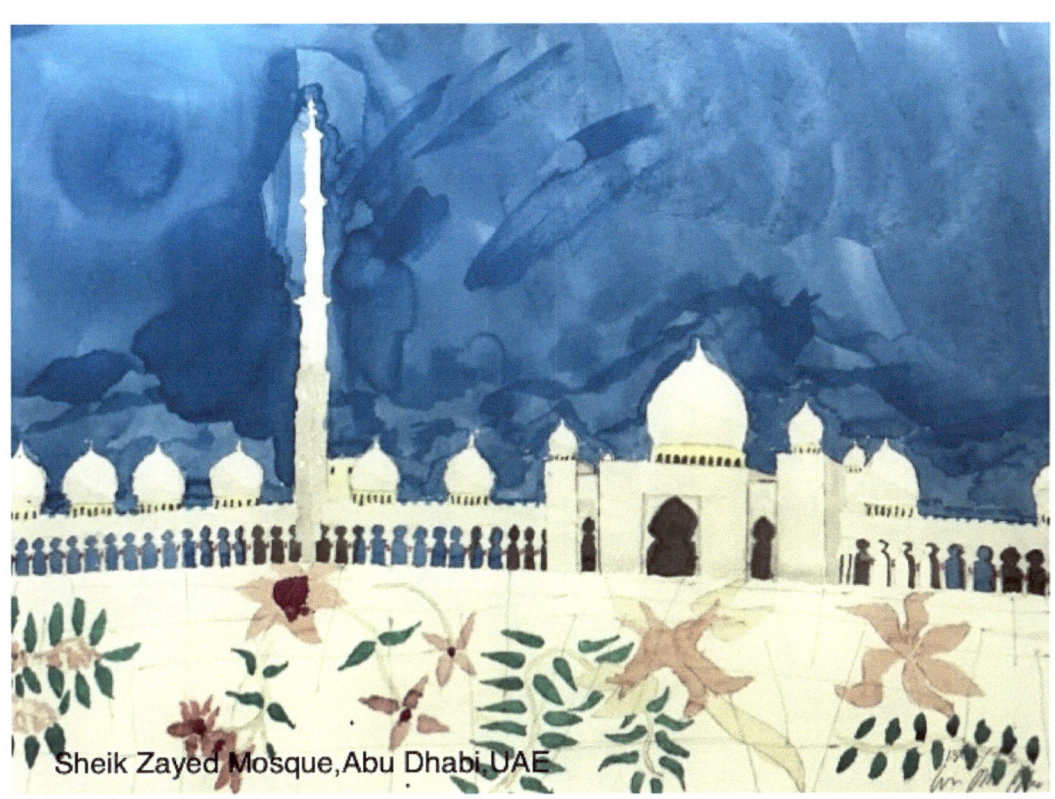

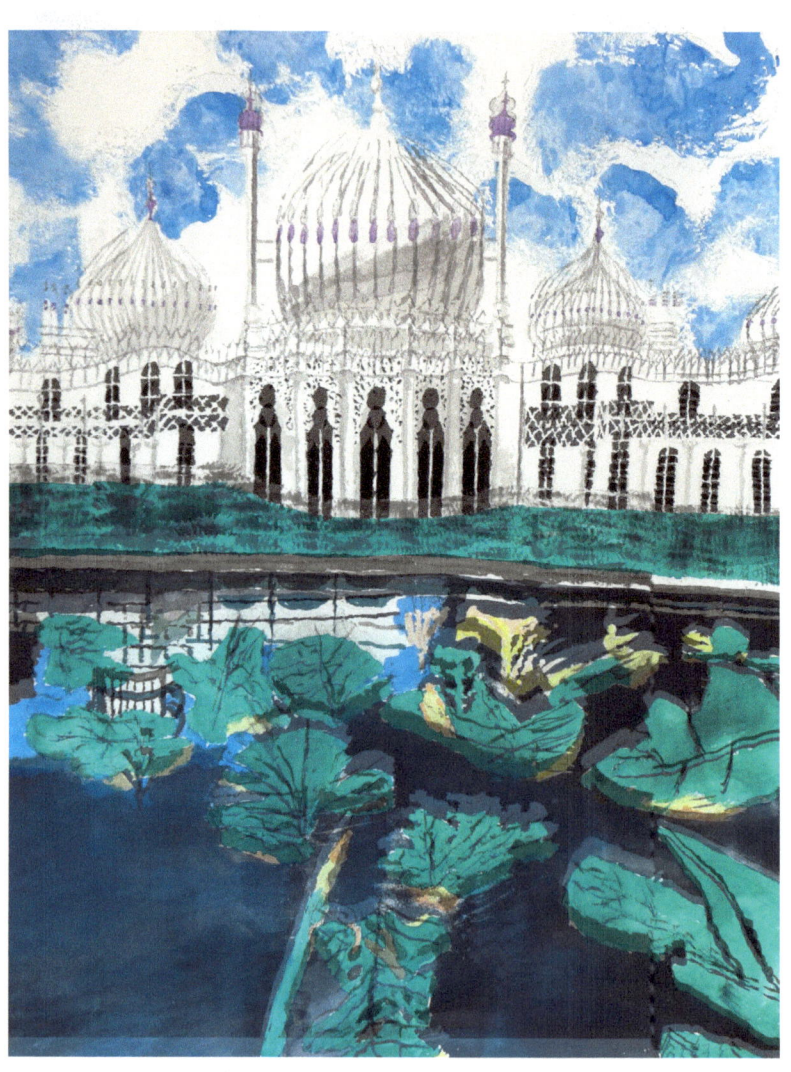

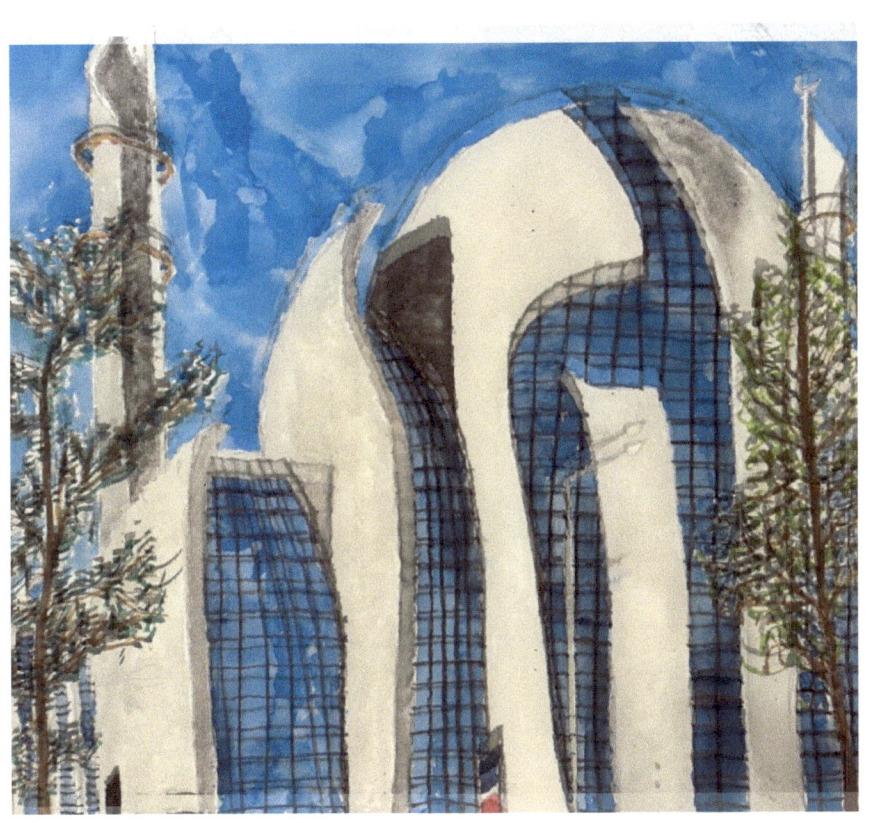

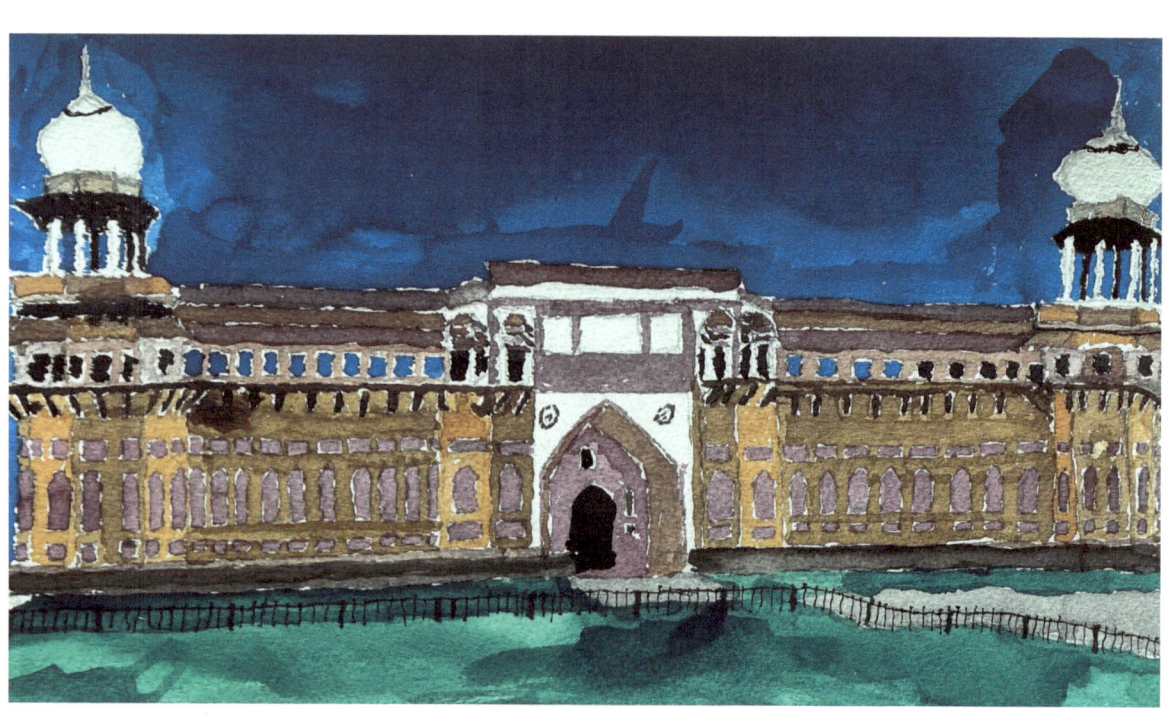

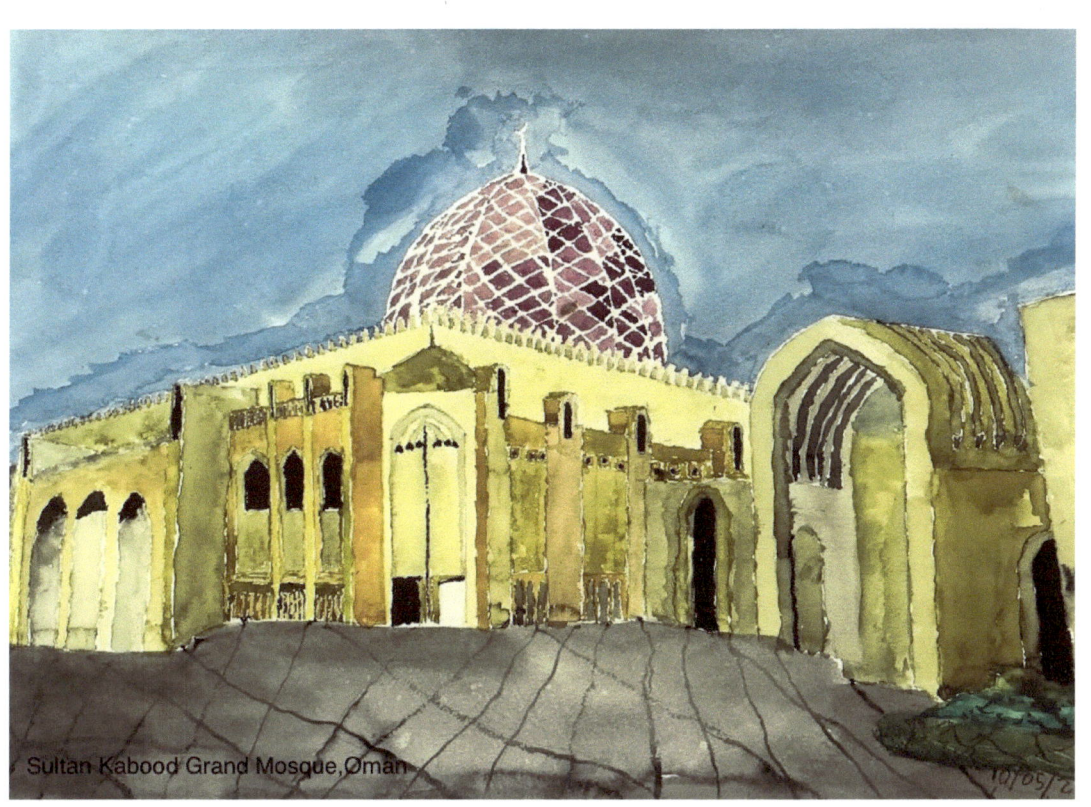

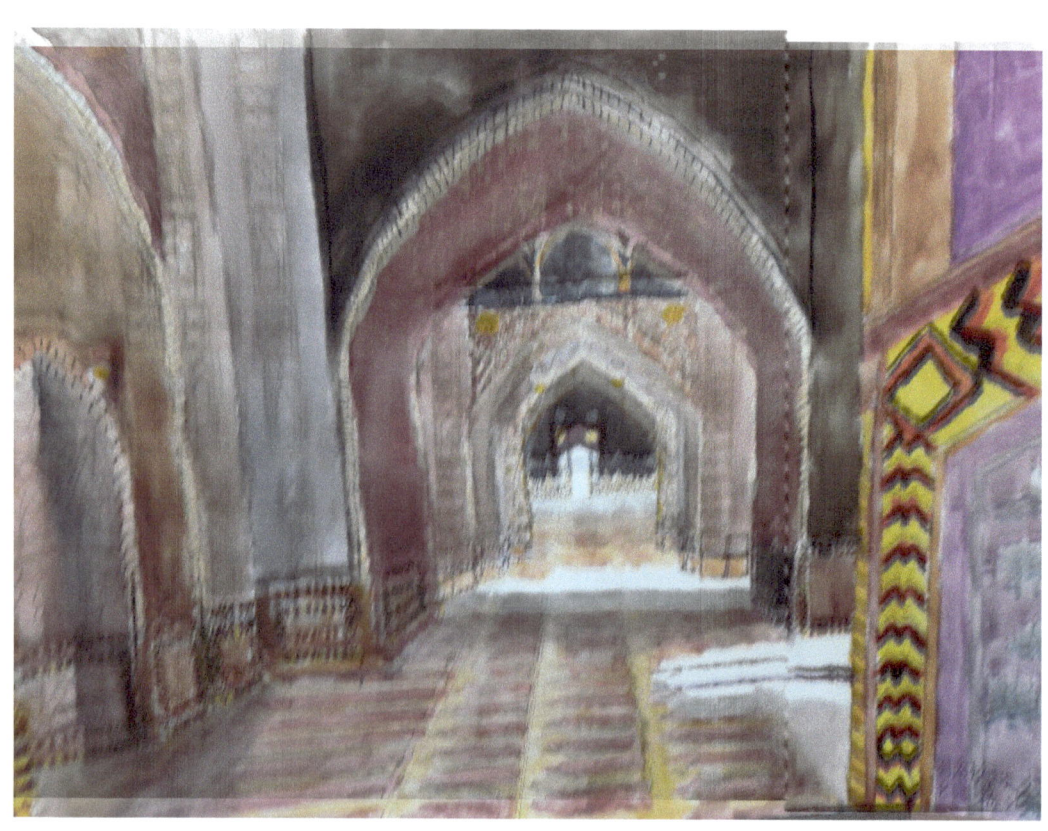

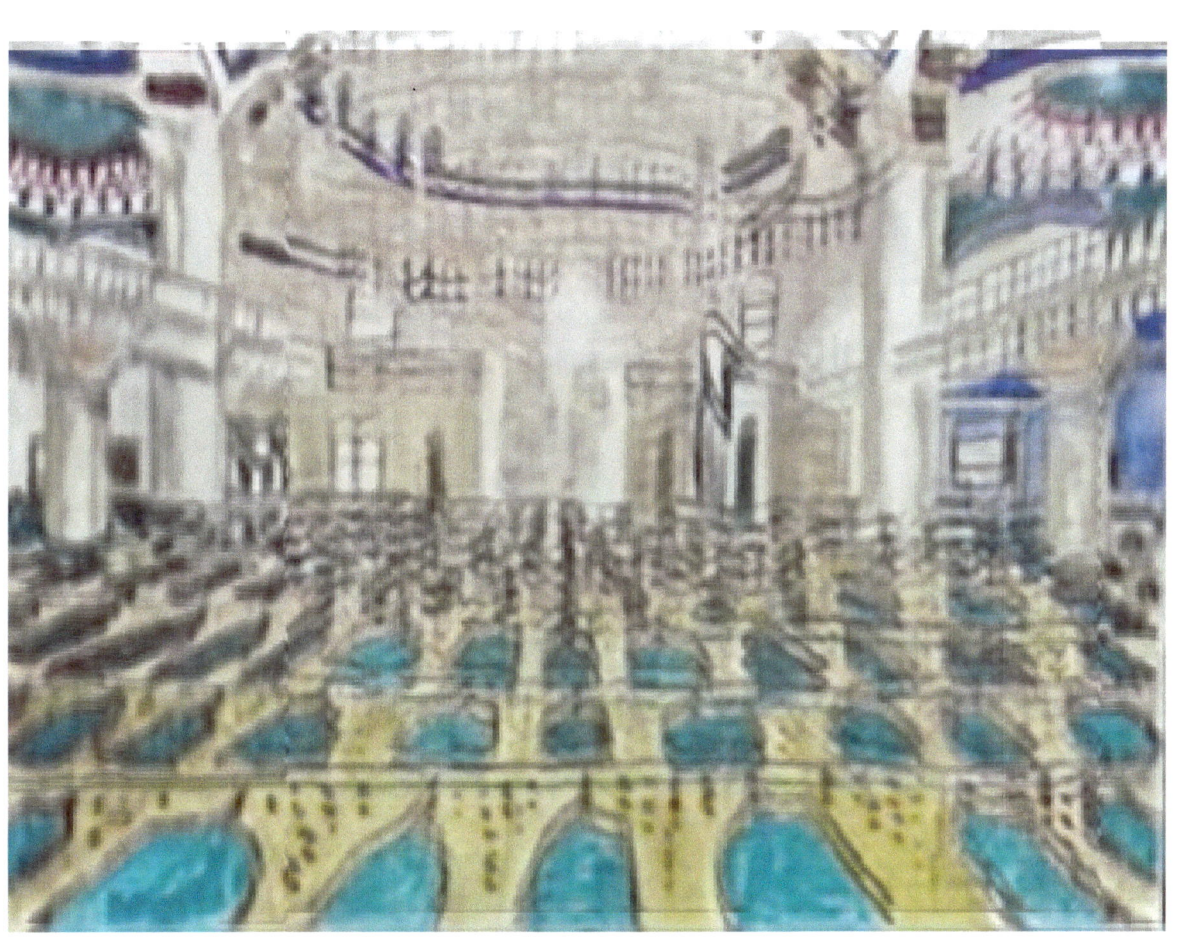

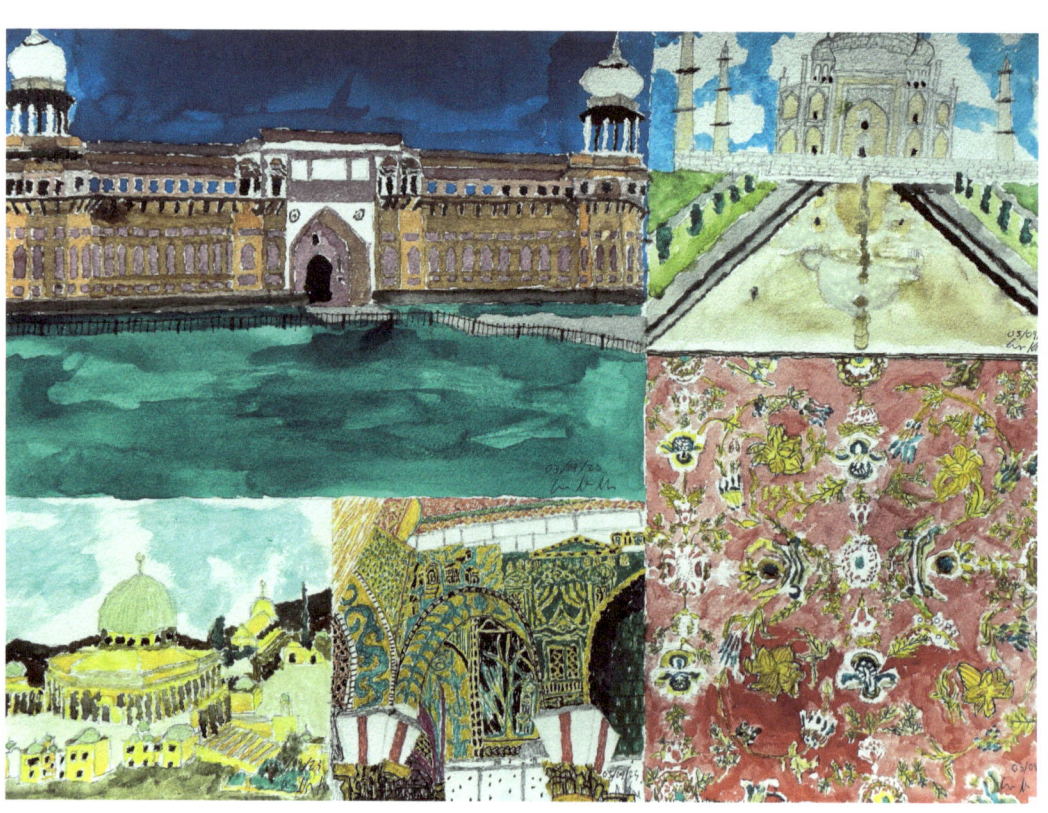

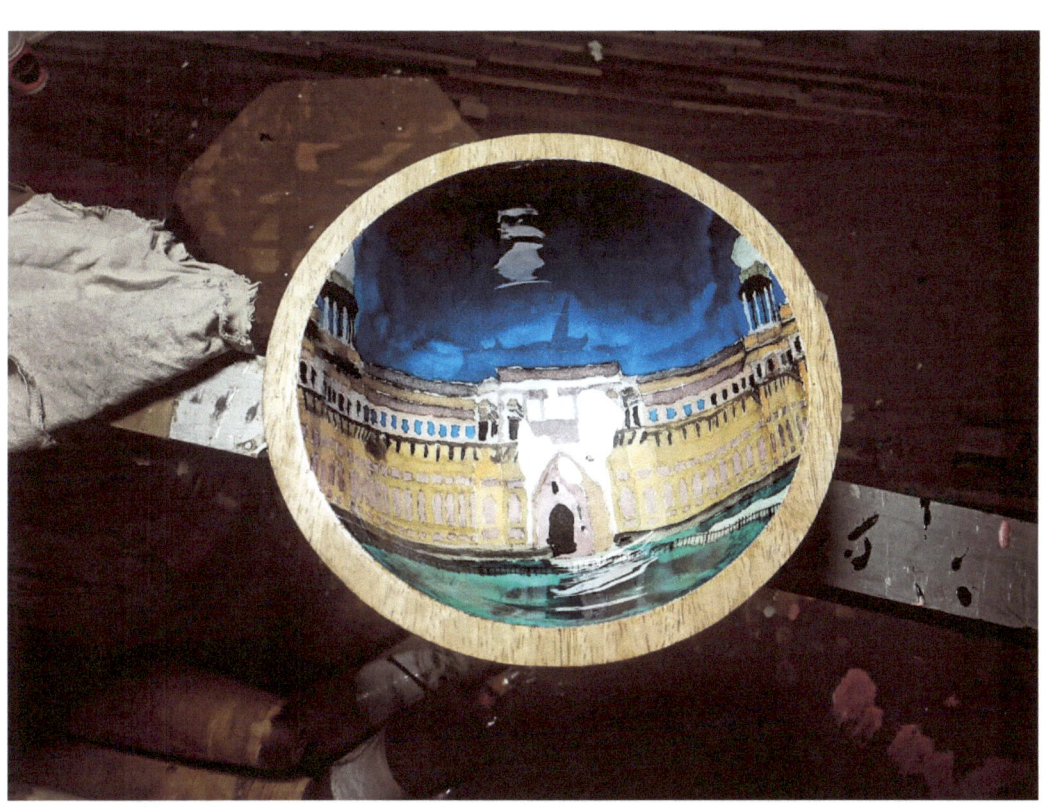

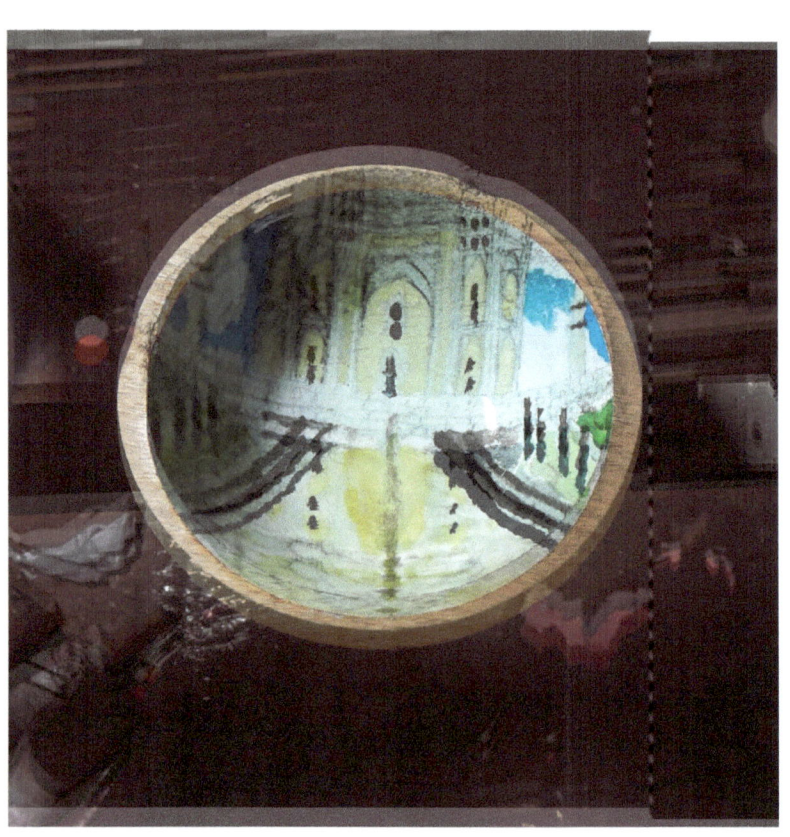

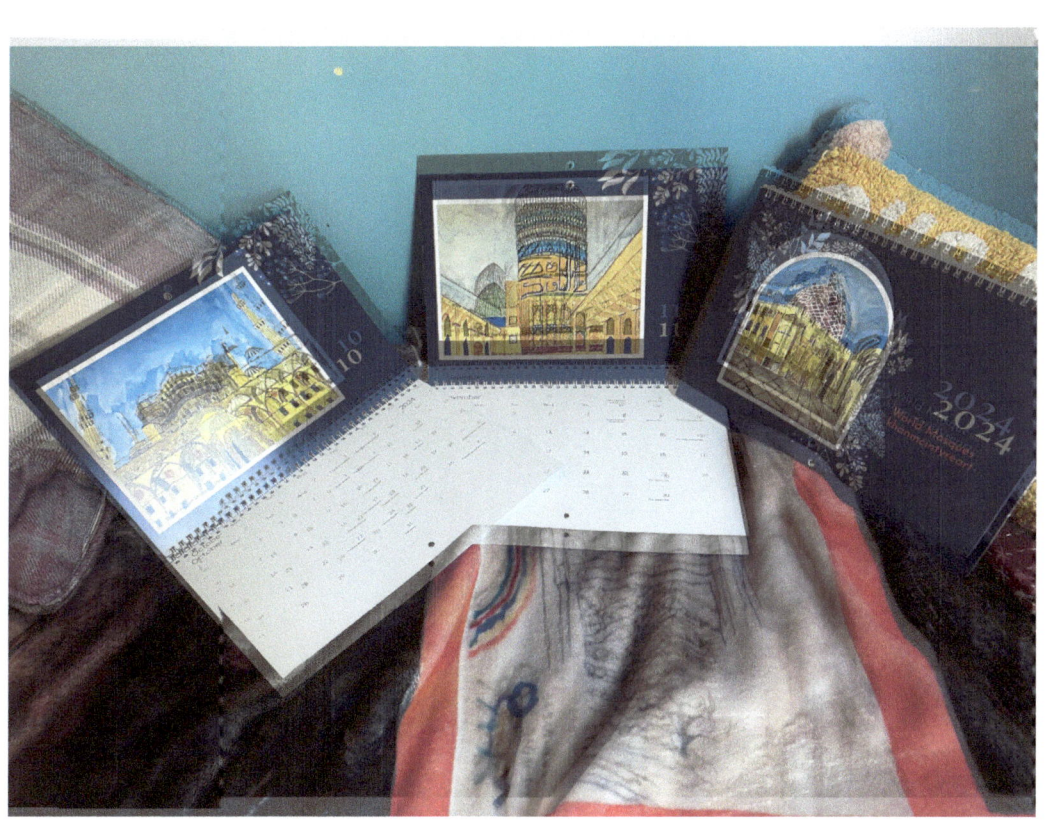

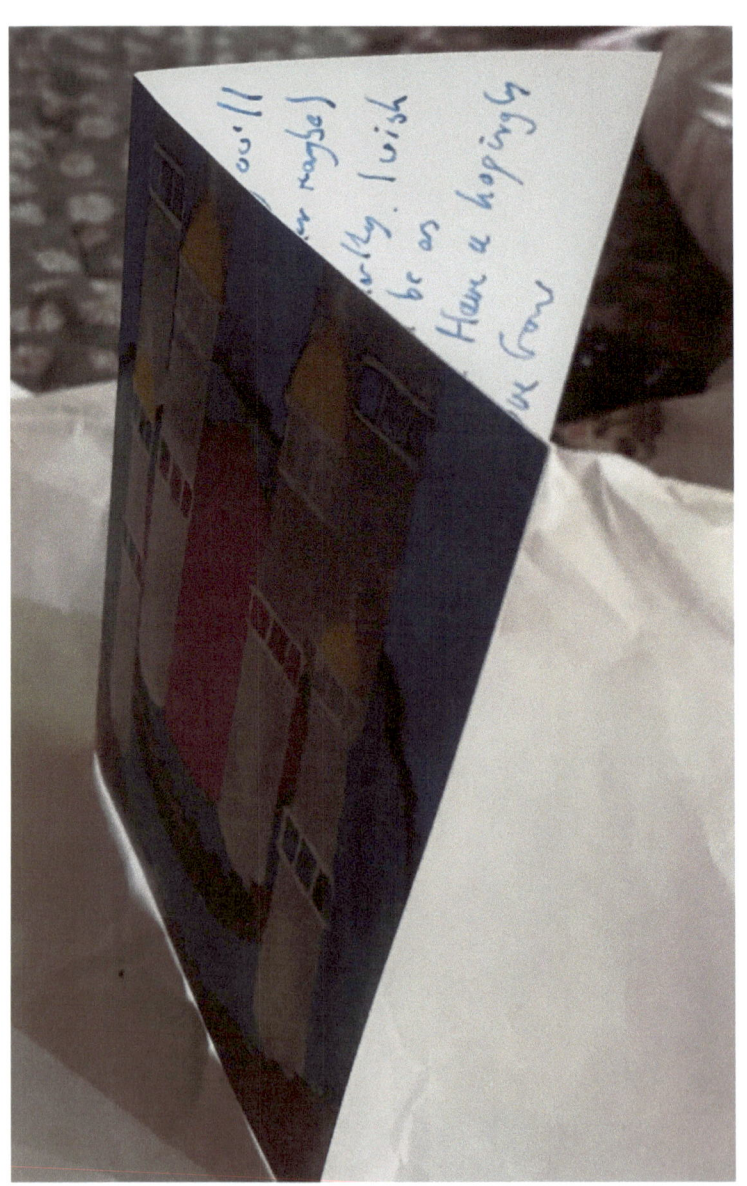

EBONY LOVE ebberscat
films Rainbow
love MEDIA books
love Publishing

khanmcintyre PICTURES
ebberscat Rainbow
FILMS love ebony BOOKS EBBERSCAT
  pictures
  ebony love love LOVE love
  LOVE
films love artwork EBONY
  ebberscat BOOKS

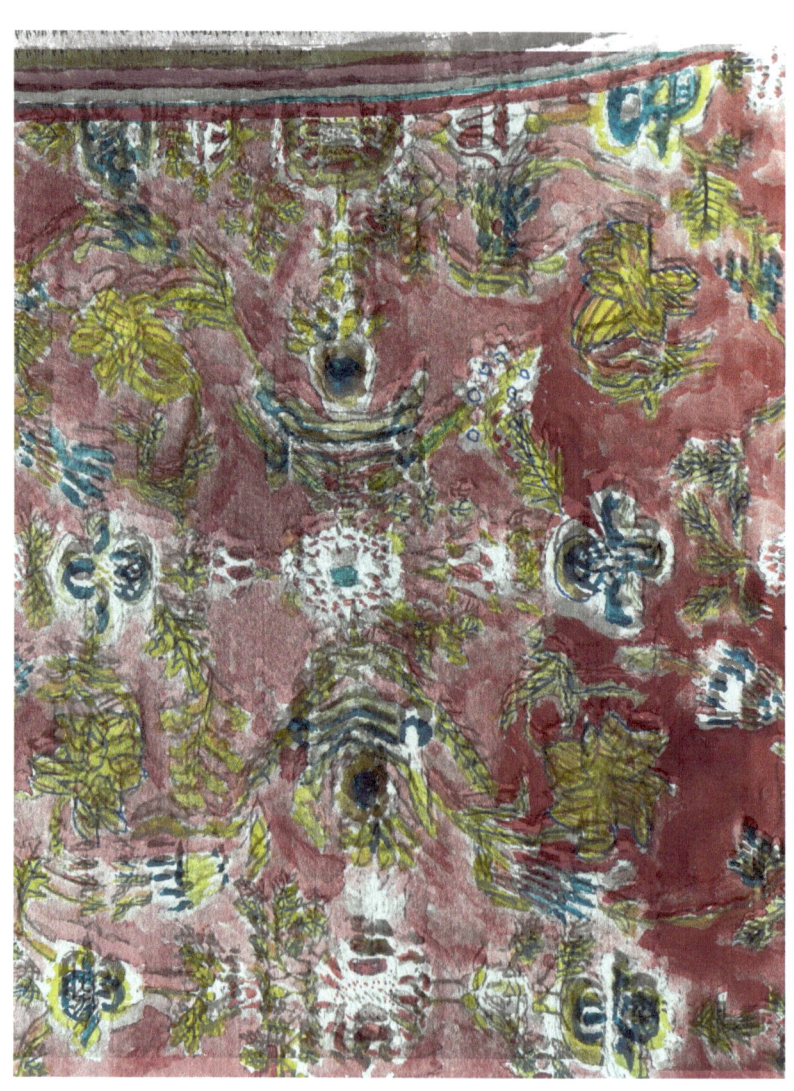

www.ingramcontent.com/pod-product-compliance
Lightning Source LLC
Chambersburg PA
CBHW051937210526
45473CB00006B/2281